ATLANTA
a celebration

PHOTOGRAPHY
CHIPP JAMISON
TEXT
BRUCE GALPHIN AND NORMAN SHAVIN
DESIGN
KATHLEEN OLDENBURG KING

International Standard Book Number 0-933238-00-2
Library of Congress Catalogue Card No. 78-71234

Copyright 1978 by Publisher: Perry Communications, Inc.
2181 Sylvan Road, SW
Atlanta, Georgia 30344

Printer: Perry Communications, Inc.

First Edition/First Printing: November, 1978
Second Printing: November, 1978

ATLANTA: A Celebration was conceived and supervised by the Special Projects Division of Perry Communications, Inc.

A new day dawns at Hartsfield International Airport.

Georgia Plaza Park, with bank towers (First National, NBG), Immaculate Conception Church

4

TIME TO CELEBRATE

ATLANTA WAS

. . . forested wilderness bordering the Creek and Cherokee Indian nations.

. . . southern anchor of a State-financed link when America began forging its web of railroads.

. . . supply depot and weapons-maker for the Confederacy.

. . . charred but undaunted victim of Gen. Sherman's incendiary March to the Sea.

. . . epitome of the phoenix legend, reborn from the ashes, a booming rail center, traveling salesmen's base, post-bellum capital of Georgia.

. . . shopping center and conversation piece for rural Georgians, with streetcars and electric lights and buildings so tall they needed elevators.

. . . restless nest-builder, migrating from West End to Inman Park to Ansley Park, Druid Hills, the Northside and suburbia in search of the ideal neighborhood.

. . . ambitious job-seeker, mounting a successful 1920s drive for regional administrative offices and manufacturing plants of national corporations.

. . . focus of Margaret Mitchell's best-selling *Gone With the Wind,* and limelighted stage for the movie's 1939 premiere.

. . . news phenomenon of the 1960s, growing from regional to national stature, raising innovative structures to an ever-altering skyline; heeding its own prophets like Dr. Martin Luther King Jr. and editor Ralph McGill to follow a path of racial progress.

ATLANTA IS

. . . physically unbounded metropolitan area, sprawling over 15 counties in the hilly Piedmont, the land rising toward the Blue Ridge Mountains.

. . . energetic hub: of transportation, business, education, government, communications; with an international airport soon to be the world's busiest; second home of most Fortune 500 firms; main office of The Coca-Cola Company, Delta Airlines and a growing galaxy of national corpora-

tions; capital of Georgia and regional sub-capital.

. . . architectural trend-setter: known not just for the atrium lobbies, soaring cylinders, triangular corners and bared-skeleton roofs, but for the multi-purpose centers and megastructures which have made Atlanta's downtown dynamic when others' have grown weary.

. . . convention capital: with its versatile new World Congress Center and convenient cluster of downtown hotels, America's number-two-ranking city in conventions booked—and aiming for number-one.

. . . magnet for the young, seeking opportunity and excitement, and by their presence enhancing both: enriching the work force, supporting a subculture of casual living, singles apartments, discos, rock concerts and the traditional arts.

. . . patron of the arts, from formal to improvisational: theater, symphony, painting, opera, chorus and dance.

. . . enthusiast for sports, spectator and participation, amateur and professional—win, lose or draw.

. . . ethnically diverse community, with American-born whites and blacks increasingly joined by Europeans, Asians, Latin Americans and Africans.

. . . gentle climate, early to Spring and late to Winter, with altitude enough to moderate its southern latitudes in Summer; usually sunny, but moist enough to mantle the region in green.

This book is about the "is" Atlanta, with a few glimpses of the "was" which remains. Here is contemporary Atlanta, comprehensively captured: its face, its livelihoods, its pleasures, its industry, its art, its setting—seen through the extraordinary vision of Chipp Jamison's lens. Brief lines identify the scenes, with more detail in the final two pages. But the real story is in the photographs. *ATLANTA: A Celebration* testifies vividly how well Jamison has learned his art and seen his adopted city.

Above all this book celebrates those who have shaped this special place, and does so with unrestrained affection.

THE NATURE OF ATLANTA

Follow Georgia from its blue foot in the Atlantic and its resin-scented southern pine woods, upward through a belt where cotton once ruled the economy and the society. By the time you reach Atlanta, the red-stained land is gently folding and rising its way to the Blue Ridge Mountains, southernmost of the Appalachian spine.

In hilly Atlanta, elevation averages 1,050 feet above sea level—barely a fifth of mile-high Denver's, but still second highest among America's major cities.

That's more than a statistic: It's a climate-molder. In Summer the height moderates the heat which Atlanta's latitude might otherwise ignite. And even when days are hot, cooling breezes wipe the brow of evening.

Atlanta's height and site make weather prediction at times a roll of the dice. Just a slight shift in weather systems, and Arctic masses may knife down from the Plains, or moist Gulf air bounce against the backboard of the hills.

Seasons are distinct, though not extreme: Winters are chill and leafless. Infrequently, a Winter's rain and freezing temperatures dress Atlanta's beloved trees in fanciful filigrees of ice and make glass of neighborhood avenues. Snow comes seldom enough to draw Atlantans outside to gawk at Nature's joke on the Sunbelt; yet it makes chaos of traffic on those one or two days a year when it strikes.

Shivering gold forsythia and violet hyacinths announce Spring before it really arrives; white and pink dogwoods and splendid many-hued azaleas confirm its entrance.

Greens deepen in Summer, and gardens rush to bloom as reward to those who have tended them with consummate patience.

In Autumn streets become cathedral naves and trees their stained-glass windows: a warm spectrum of crimsons, clarets and golds.

Not a single peachtree grows along Peachtree, Atlanta's most famous street. The species is not indigenous, though some can be nurtured to survive the cool Winters. The name derives from a Creek Indian village named Standing Peachtree, but no one is certain whether it was a peachtree at that 18th Century camp or a pitch (resin) tree: a pine.

The region's bountiful rivers, streams, and lakes are fed by ample rain: about 48 inches in a typical year; late Winter is the wettest season, Autumn the driest.

Atlantans are jealous of the greenery these waters nourish. They bemoan the wrenching up of trees for the region's remarkable decades of growth. But to the visitor's eye, Atlanta remains a marvel of vegetation, with great mature trees casting their canopies not only over suburban homes but even into the pulsing heart of the city.

Atlanta was born in a forest and those who have made it home have strived to maintain Nature's first design, yet harmonize it with man's inner urging to build ever more stately mansions.

And if you wish to recapture a sense of the Atlanta as it appeared to its earliest pioneers, glimpse it from the air: It still resembles a vast forest, Nature's own celebration.

Morning mist . . . on the Chattahoochee River

. . . and over the spire-pierced canopy of trees in Buckhead

The "Dogwood City's" favorite trees flaunt their colors.

The seasons in Atlanta: multicolored Spring azaleas

. . . Summer ferns and trees

12

. . . the Joseph's coat of Autumn maples

. . . and eerie patterns of rare Winter ice

13

Atlantans enjoy outdoors most of the year

. . . and so do marigolds.

14

Autumn weaves a subtle tapestry.

CITYSCAPES

Gen. Sherman couldn't hold a candle to the destruction Atlantans themselves have wrought on their architectural heritage. Until about a decade ago, the controlling consensus was that new meant progress and old meant antiquated. In a city with as much hustle as Atlanta, it's not surprising that the best-preserved area from early days is a cemetery.

If the fabric is thin at the ante-bellum end of the tapestry, at least there are some threads: Tullie Smith House, an uncolumned "plantation plain" farm home typical of the 1840s, moved to the Atlanta Historical Society grounds from DeKalb acreage now occupied by an office park; Anthony's Restaurant, built around a plantation house brought from Greenville, Ga.; and the Historic Roswell district, a few miles north of downtown Atlanta, a jewel box of authentic ante-bellum homes and shops.

The preservation spirit took root in Atlanta in time to save and restore significant enclaves and individual examples of its Victorian past: Inman Park, once the domain of Atlanta's elite, later a slum, now again a vital community; West End, especially around Peeples and Oglethorpe Streets, with handsomely restored bungalows; the Peters House, occupying a prime in-town block, currently a restaurant appropriately called The Mansion; and the Wren's Nest, also in West End, author Joel Chandler Harris' home and now a museum of his Uncle Remus creations.

Commercial buildings do not arouse the same passion as homes, so look quickly lest the Victorian and turn-of-the-century stores in "The Gulch" south of Five Points disappear under MARTA subway construction and the commercial development which tracks its completion.

Time moves more calmly in Oakland Cemetery, which is almost as old as the city. Though continually in need of restoration funds, it has preserved in monuments and markers the tastes of bygone eras. Its largely Victorian sculpture may be too sweetly sentimental for today's tastes, but their charm is inescapable.

The Candler Building, with its handsome marble and bronze sculpture and detailing, is a well preserved memorial to the growing economic muscle of 1906 Atlanta, and especially of the Coca-Cola wealth which built it.

The automobile expanded Atlanta's frontiers in the Twenties, opening Buckhead and miles of the Northside, with their spacious lawns and homes modeled on older European styles. Architect Philip Shutze's Swan House, now part of the Atlanta Historical Society complex, is the apotheosis of this classical thrust.

Art Deco reigned only a few years and was further pinched by the Great Depression, but Atlanta has a few survivors of the restrained geometric ornamentation: The William-Oliver Building at Five Points, William Orr Doctor's Building, the older portion of Southern Bell's Ivy Street Building.

The Fox Theatre is unique, the last hurrah of the Silver Screen era, a fantasy inspired by Egyptian and Middle Eastern themes.

Contemporary Atlanta architecture and urban design are trend-setters. John Portman's Regency, with its roof-high lobby, revolutionized American hotel design. Peachtree Center, the Omni complex and Colony Square all have attracted international attention for gathering multiple activities within a single group of buildings or megastructures. Atlanta is learning that urban design is not merely structures, but their interplay with parks, outdoor sculpture, "urban walls"—and people. A distinct "Atlanta feeling" is emerging from the melding of many parts.

"Plantation plain" Tullie Smith House

In West End, a revival

In Oakland Cemetery, 19th Century sentiment preserved

. . . for the vanquished Confederacy

. . . and a praying child

Restoration in Victorian Inman Park

Georgia's gilded Capitol dome

. . . and the Hall of Flags inside

21

Staircase in the opulent Candler Building

. . . and the ornate facade

Exterior of classic Swan House

. . . and its formal period decor at Atlanta Historical Society

Circular Hall, Governor's Mansion

. . . and mirror-reflected guest bedroom

Echoes of Italy: Villa Apartments

Northside living: a quiet elegance

25

The Fox, rare survivor among movie palaces: Moorish arches

. . . a ladies' lounge

. . . and the familiar sign by night

Southern Bell belle

. . . and Art Deco elevator doors, Orr Building

The lobby that revolutionized hotel design: Hyatt Regency

Peachtree Center: a city within the city

. . . dining in its open patio

. . . and in its shopping mall

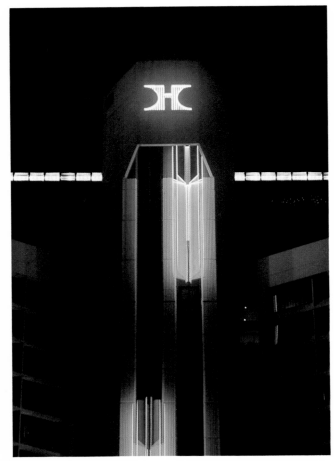

The Hilton's exterior elevators

The Plaza's massive columns and interior lake

Peachtree Summit: bold use of triangular site

A handsome couple: Central City Park, Trust Company Bank

Lighted fountains grace Georgia Power's entrance.

Omni International's many-faceted atrium

Omni complex, Coliseum in foreground

North Avenue vista includes Tech, office towers, apartments.

Reflections at sundown: Tower Place

The Colony Square micropolis

Dining on its "Town Square"

36

Shopping malls: Lenox Square sculpture

. . . and Perimeter's mobiles

In the suburbs, office parks (Perimeter Center East)

. . . and contemporary-style living (Joe Amisano residence)

At sunset, the ever-changing downtown skyline

ATLANTA AT WORK

Official statistics capture the numbers but not the character of what Atlantans do for a living. Officially, the largest employment categories, in descending order, are: wholesale/retail trade, service jobs, industry, government.

By employee headcount, transportation ranks further down the list. But transportation—specifically railroads—gave birth to Atlanta, and a full range of movement modes make everything else happen in the Metro region today.

Atlanta is wholesale/retail sales center, regional headquarters for business and the Federal government, America's second most active convention city, capital of Georgia, communications control point, and financial center because it is so easy to get to. Hartsfield International Airport is the world's second busiest airport, and by the early 1980s, after completion of a new terminal, it will rank first. It offers nonstop flights to Europe, the Caribbean, Mexico and virtually all population centers of the United States. Six interstate highway legs, tied together with a suburban belt, converge just below the Capitol; they serve not only local and through passengers, but a major trucking industry. Rails no longer carry the great passenger volume of earlier days, but Atlanta's freight lines web the compass.

Combined with an appealing climate, productive labor pool, sound governments, moderate cost of living, and abundant entertainment and cultural amenities, this transportation web makes Metro Atlanta a logical place to base regional sales forces, administer Federal programs for the Southeast, hold trade shows, headquarter trucking lines, warehouse goods, etc.

Homebred and transplant, growing numbers of national and international businesses are making Metro Atlanta their headquarters. Among the largest are The Coca-Cola Company, Delta Air Lines, Gold Kist Inc., Fuqua Industries, National Service Industries, Simmons Company, Oxford Industries, Royal Crown Cola, E. T. Barwick Industries, Neptune International, Cagles Inc., The Southern Company and Continental Telephone Company.

As a regional financial capital, Atlanta is headquarters of the Sixth District Federal Reserve Bank and the Big Five commercial banks: Citizens & Southern, First National, Trust Company of Georgia, Fulton National and National Bank of Georgia. Atlanta is home of Life Insurance Company of Georgia and Atlanta Life, one of the nation's largest black-owned insurance companies.

Such activities demand seas of typists, clerks, statisticians, construction and maintenance workers, drivers, salesmen, junior executives, waiters, hotel employees. Jobs generate more jobs: for entertainers, teachers, printers, computer programmers, chefs, investment brokers, market researchers, social workers, models, newscasters.

High skill, low skill. Old hand, neophyte. Generalist, specialist. Ivy League, Good Ol' Boy. Atlanta is a magnet whose reputation has drawn talents from all parts of the country.

Railroading, Atlanta's first industry (Inman Yards)

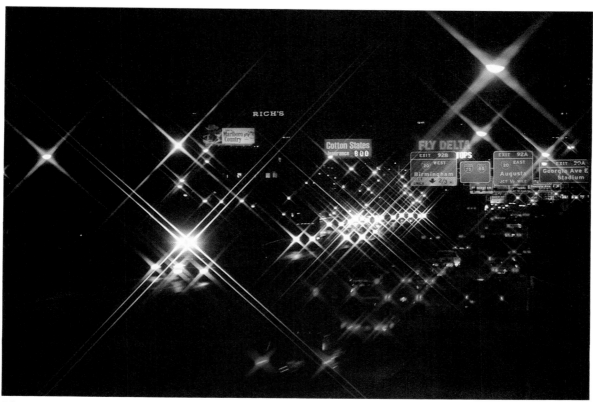

Three Interstate highways converge below Capitol: view by night

. . . and by day, from overhead.

At busy Hartsfield, a waiting line of jets

Overhaul at Delta maintenance base

Control tower of world's second busiest airport

Man's face shows jet engine's scale.

Movement means mass numbers: trucks

. . . automobiles in a parking lot

. . . and MARTA buses at Pine Street yard.

Atlanta is a financial capital (lobby, C&S main bank)

. . . and fashion center (models after show).

Representatives of Fire Bureau

. . . Bureau of Police Services

. . . and Center for Disease Control: Government is major employer.

48

Farmers Market: reminder of Georgia's agricultural past—and present

At the Flea Market, a bit of everything

Lockheed-Georgia is famous for heavy-hauling planes.

Huge spools of cable at Western Electric

Atlanta is home for the logo seen round the world.

Independent bottlers buy syrup from The Coca-Cola Company.

Superheated metal sprays sparks at Atlantic Steel.

Rapid transit comes to Atlanta: new rail cars

. . . and construction of huge ▶
Five Points station

Food service vital to hotels, conventions (Bugatti buffet table)

Catering a large banquet at the Hilton

57

Atlanta's international convention draw is growing.

Annual Bobbin Show fills exhibit hall

. . . and rest of World Congress Center.

Above pool, the towering column of Peachtree Plaza

ATLANTA AT PLAY

From pioneer reminiscences, frontier Atlanta's earliest sport may have been the barroom brawl. But even before "Terminus" became its unofficial name, before there was a municipal government or a church, citizens began to organize their recreation.

A Mrs. Mulligan, wife of a railroad construction foreman, probably was Atlanta's first informal commissioner of cultural affairs: She hosted a celebrative "ball" after the dirt floor of the Mulligan shack was covered with planks.

It has never taken much prodding to engage Atlantans in sports and recreation. As early as 1866 the Atlanta Baseball Club was organized and soon thereafter, a rival team was formed: the Gate City Nine. After the Gate City Nine whipped the older Club 127 to 29, the losing team soon disbanded.

But Atlanta has had inter-city baseball since the 1880s when editor Henry Grady promoted the Southern League. Georgia Tech introduced a regular football season soon after its founding in the 1880s and Atlantans pack college and professional stadiums even in losing years. Grand-slammer Bobby Jones enshrined golf in the hearts of even the highest-scoring duffers. Bitsy Grant and Louise Suggs similarly popularized tennis.

Today Atlanta offers a splashy spectrum of sports, Big League and amateur, professionally packed and chaotically eccentric, team and individual, spectator and participation.

It is local lore that in the mid-1960s some Atlantans began planning a stadium on land they didn't own with money they didn't have to attract a baseball team they didn't get. But they did build a stadium to seat more than 55,000, and they did get a team, the Braves. In short order there followed Big League football (Falcons), basketball (Hawks) and hockey (Flames), the last two in yet another new 17,000-seat arena, the Omni.

Near Atlanta are two nationally recognized auto racecourses, Road Atlanta and Atlanta International Raceway. The Atlanta Athletic Club course is on the Professional Golf Association tour. Atlanta's annual Hunt Meet and Steeplechase and the Hunter-Jumper Classic grow in size and stature every year.

But commercial competitions are only one measure of Atlanta's sports devotion. Parks sprout almost as many teams as dogwoods: amateur league and spur-of-the-moment. Joggers pace streets from dawn to dusk. Public golf and tennis courts have waiting lines in all but rainy and freezing weather. Nearby Lake Lanier makes landlocked Atlanta one of the boating capitals of America. Indoor ice skating, polo, soccer, racquetball, ballooning—all have well organized devotees.

If a sport like rugby is too exotic for professional competition, it still draws determined amateurs. Occasionally Atlanta adds its own touch to recognized sports, such as the annual Spring free-for-all: the Great Race on the Chattahoochee River, certified by Guinness as the world's biggest participation sports event.

Recreation has gone Big League in recent years. Atlantans as early as the 1880s and 1890s showed their fascination with large-scale amusements by sponsoring three national and international fairs. But in the 1950s, there was little to show a visitor but the Grant Park Zoo, Lake Spivey, the Battle of Atlanta Cyclorama and the unfinished carving on Stone Mountain.

Atlanta's growth in size and diversity, however, and its booming convention and tourism business created a market for major family attractions: Six Flags Over Georgia, Stone Mountain Park and Kingdoms 3. Underground Atlanta, which survived a near-fatal body blow from rapid-transit construction, continues to attract.

In the past decade, Atlanta's restaurant industry has taken quantum leaps in culinary variety, sophistication and luxury. With the last vestiges of Prohibition-era mores fading, a colorful nightlife has blossomed.

From chic to bawdy, from elegant to eccentric, the Big A is alive—and celebrating.

Atlanta offers diversions for all ages, from skate-boarding

. . . to a country hoedown on Peachtree Street.

There's rafting on the Chattahoochee River

. . . sailing on Lanier (above) and other lakes

. . . and golf just about everywhere (here, Lake Lanier Islands).

You can stress yourself as a participant

. . . or whoop it up as a spectator

. . . at events like Road Atlanta races.

You can just sit and watch (Barn Dinner Theatre)

. . . or join in the swing of things (Burt's Place, Omni International).

The Metro area has three theme parks: Kingdoms 3

. . . Stone Mountain attractions include steamboat, among many rides

. . . and high-relief memorial sculpture

*. . . and breath-taking rides
at Six Flags Over Georgia.*▶

Stadium above is home of Braves, Falcons; Hawks, Flames play at Omni (p. 34)

Braves are Atlanta's oldest Big League team

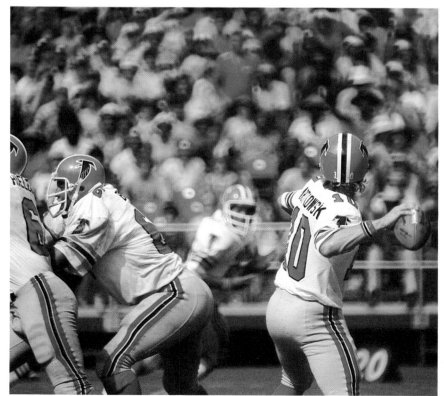

The National Football League Falcons in action

. . . and in time out.

The Flames, here on Omni ice, are Atlanta's youngest pro team.

Steeplechase (above), Hunter-Jumper Classic are annual horse events.

Dante's Down the Hatch, Underground Atlanta's best known attraction

Greenhouse in Piedmont Park, site of proposed botanical gardens

MIND AND SPIRIT

In 1847, when Atlanta was chartered as a city, a newly arrived teacher complained that "Atlanta now contains 2,000 inhabitants, yet everyone does what is right in his own eyes. [The settlement has little government and] no church and little preaching."

Those omissions were on the way to remedying. In December of that year the Legislature granted a municipal charter, a few months after a combination school and church building had been built by public subscription.

Soon the variety of Atlantans' religious persuasions became more visible. In 1848 Methodists, Episcopalians and Baptists built churches, and a Presbyterian congregation was organized. Roman Catholics raised their first sanctuary in 1851, and Jews organized their first congregation in 1867.

From the beginning, religious organization went hand in hand with stability in the community. The rowdy spirit spawned in the railroad camp of Terminus did not disappear overnight with emergence of churches, but the more settled citizens soon gained control in young Atlanta.

Higher education in Atlanta, too, was nurtured in the womb of religion. The city's oldest institution in continuous operation, Atlanta University, was chartered in 1867 and launched for the benefit of former slaves with funds from the Freedman's Bureau and the American Missionary Assn. All five other institutions in the predominantly black Atlanta University Center also have church roots: Spelman (Baptist, with a substantial infusion of Rockefeller money), Morehouse (American Baptist Home Mission Board), Morris Brown (African Methodist Episcopal), Clark (Methodist Episcopal) and Interdenominational Theological Seminary.

The AU institutions have had enormous impact on contemporary American life: A great number of the nation's black leaders are graduates.

In terms of its birth date, Presbyterian-founded Oglethorpe University could claim to be Atlanta's senior institution of higher learning, but as presently constituted it opened in 1916. Agnes Scott College in Decatur, still all-female, also was born of the Presbyterian Church (in 1891).

Emory College, Methodist-related, moved from Oxford, Ga., to Atlanta in 1919 and has grown—with the generosity of two Coca-Cola families, Candler and Woodruff—into a highly ranked university and medical center.

Not all of Metro Atlanta's higher education institutions are church-related, of course. Today there are 29 degree-granting colleges, junior colleges and universities, including two major State of Georgia institutions, the Georgia Institute of Technology and Georgia State University. The former, as its name implies, specializes in engineering and the physical sciences. GSU is especially strong in business administration and urban life studies.

Religious institutions are similarly diverse. Protestant churches are still dominant (especially Baptist and Methodist), but they are supplemented today not only by Catholic and Jewish institutions, but by more exotic religions ranging from Black Muslim to Hare Krishna.

The role of churches today continues in part what it was in early Atlanta: a stabilizing, conservative influence. But black churches in particular were an important vehicle in the Civil Rights struggles of the Fifties and Sixties, and some predominantly white, upper-middle-class churches are deeply involved in problems of the inner city.

Like Atlanta as a whole, the institutions of the mind and spirit are growing in diversity and thus in strength.

Byzantine-style mosaic icons, Greek Orthodox Cathedral of the Annunciation

Second Ponce de Leon Baptist Church, Buckhead

Classical interior of the Temple, Reform Jewish synagogue

Monastery of the Holy Ghost in Conyers

Ebenezer Baptist Church: The late Dr. Martin Luther King Jr. was co-pastor.

Dr. King's tomb with the prophetic "Free at last . . ." quote

Spires of Sacred Heart, First Methodist against Peachtree Summit facade▶

Harkness Hall, Atlanta University

Georgia State University's "concrete campus" in heart of downtown

GSU pedestrian bridges over city streets

Sun reflectors at Georgia Tech, a leader in solar energy research

The "Ramblin' Wreck" is a Tech tradition.

Woodruff Medical Center, Emory

Modern Chemistry Building at Emory University

At Fernbank Science Center, one of nation's largest urban telescopes

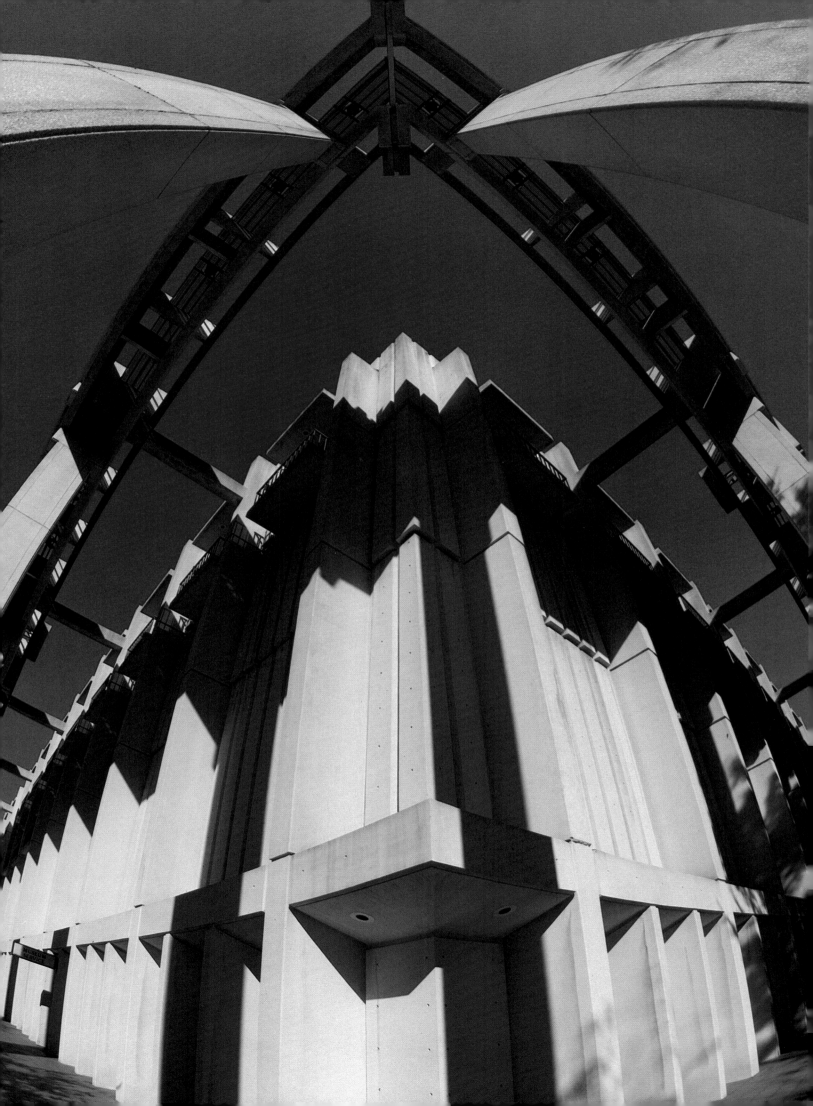

THE ART OF ATLANTA

The curtain rose at Atlanta's first regular theater, the Athenaeum, in 1855. The auditorium was relegated to the second floor above a Decatur Street grain and grocery store, but at least the theater boasted a resident family troupe.

During most of its early years, though, Atlanta depended on traveling performers and lecturers for its contact with the arts. Museums, symphony orchestras and professional acting companies are not born overnight.

Today these and many other art institutions have been born, and are alive and vigorous in Atlanta. They are undernourished for funds, but where are the arts ever elsewise?

Today's established institutions evolved from civic theaters, dance students' recitals, private art collections, a children's orchestra. Vying for their place in the limelight are the youthful challengers: experimental, improvisational, special-interest, ambitious, debt-ridden—always reaching for new glimpses of Truth and Beauty.

Most formally organized and financed are the Atlanta Arts Alliance components: High Museum of Art, Atlanta Symphony Orchestra, Alliance Theatre, Atlanta Children's Theatre and the four-year degree-granting Atlanta College of Art. Their single-roof home is Atlanta Memorial Arts Center, dedicated in 1968 to honor more than 100 local art-lovers who died in a Paris air crash six years before.

The relatively young High cannot afford the massive collections of urban museums established in the late 19th and early 20th Centuries, but has a fine, small cross section of Medieval and Renaissance art (Kress Collection), late 19th Century American oils, late 19th and early 20th Century prints (Uhrey Collection), and African and Asian art objects. It has attracted many excellent traveling shows and has mounted impressive shows of its own for local and touring exhibition.

Atlanta has become a major art market, and galleries abound. More important, art is everywhere: bank lobbies, shopping centers, even restaurant "galleries." There are colorful "urban wall" murals and ever more outdoor sculpture. The annual Piedmont Arts Festival attracts visitors from all parts of America.

Maestro Robert Shaw has developed the Atlanta Symphony Orchestra to a high polish which wins not only local but national touring applause. The Symphony Orchestra is the source of several smaller performing groups, and is supplemented at times by an outstanding Chamber Chorus. More than two dozen college, church and community musical organizations also perform regularly for the public.

In addition to Alliance Theatre, Academy Theatre is a well established company with strong educational programming and a few commissioned new plays; the Winter Play Season and (Summer) Theatre of the Stars blend recognized stars with local casts; Kelly's Feed and Seed Theatre has been perhaps the most successful of the large number of small, innovative companies; Barn Dinner Theatre and Harlequin Dinner Theatre add the pleasure of established titles to the local scene.

Atlantans are dance-lovers; several companies flourish. The Atlanta Ballet is America's oldest regional company. Southern Ballet of Atlanta also has a long, fine history. The Ruth Mitchell Dance Company, Company Kaye, Atlanta Dance Unit and Leslie Morris Dance Unit are among the best known of several other performing dance groups.

Atlantans remain hospitable to traveling artists. The Atlanta Music Club series, for example, has offered outstanding attractions for many years. And Atlantans have a special love affair with the Metropolitan Opera of New York: Except for some war and depression years, the Met has visited every Spring since 1911.

Exercises for a ballet dancer

Glass sculptor Hans Fräbel in his studio

Road to nowhere and cars going nowhere

Graphic on graphic: MARTA bus and urban wall

More exterior murals: a money theme

. . . . and flights of fancy

Participation adds to High Museum's
"Children in America" exhibit. ▶

Handsome Galleria ties together Arts Alliance components.

Maestro Robert Shaw conducting the Atlanta Symphony Orchestra

Two-towered light sculpture at Omni International

Sculpture and fountain in Midnight Sun restaurant court

Editor Henry Grady, Fulton National Bank

109

Eagle on column, Federal Reserve Bank

Woman with Phoenix, M. L. King Dr. at Spring St.

110

Homage to womanhood, Peachtree at 15th Sts.

A MECCA FOR PEOPLE

Day by day they arrive, the new citizens of Metro Atlanta—more every year than live in Georgia's ninth largest city. Population of the 15 Metro counties exceeds 1.75 million, and not even a quarter are locally born.

Who are they, where do they come from, and what draws them here?

Atlanta remains a regional mecca: Most newcomers come from the Southeast, following the traditional American pattern of seeking opportunity near one's roots. But the whole answer is that they come from everywhere—not just the rest of America, but in booming numbers, from the rest of the world.

Why they come is simple to explain. Why they *stay* says something special about Atlanta.

Since its birth, Atlanta has had a reputation for hustle and bustle, for growth, for pursuing the unlikely—and achieving it. Atlanta was barely 10 years out of its railroad-camp womb when it proposed itself as the capital of Georgia, and 21 years later—in 1868—it was.

In the 1960s, Atlanta advertised itself as no longer a merely regional capital but as a great national city. Imperceptibly, with no specific date to mark the achievement, it was so recognized by the rest of America.

In the early 1970s, with little to prove its point, it boasted that it was "the world's next great city." The goal comes closer daily—one international flight, one European bank office, one new consulate, one new foreign business tie, one burgeoning ethnic enclave at a time.

Each newcomer has sampled Atlanta or gotten the word—from friend, relative, newspaper and magazine article—that Atlanta is a city of work opportunity, of open-mindedness, hospitality and tolerance, a city that encourages creativity, a city of good climate and good times.

Many come because their companies send them to staff and manage the regional offices here. Their Atlanta performances are sometimes out-of-town tryouts for the Broadways of their careers. But a funny thing happens on the way to the big forum: Thousands fall in love with Atlanta, and change their jobs if necessary to stay.

Such a city naturally appeals especially to the young and ambitious. Not surprisingly, the average age is lower—by nearly two years—in Metro Atlanta than in America as a whole.

Ethnically, Metro Atlanta is more than three fourths white. Blacks are in a majority within the City of Atlanta. Within the Metro area as a whole, black-white ratios have changed little in past decades.

The most noticeable new trend is the growing infusion of foreign-born: refugees of political upheavals, employees of overseas companies expanding into the Southeast, and individuals seeking opportunity in a city of proven promise. They add new flavors to Atlanta: ethnic restaurants and grocery stores, occasionally exotic costumes, festivals, and music; bilingual signs for banks, international symbols at Hartsfield Atlanta International Airport and on the highways, foreign-language news broadcasts and TV shows.

With the increasing diversity of Atlanta's people, the city's character and its cultural mix alter continually. And the allure grows stronger.

Study in youth and age: reading at Colony Square

. . . and enjoying coffee and cigarette

The Municipal Market

. . . has views resembling

. . . a miniature United Nations.

More contrasts: fur-coated luxury shopping

. . . and celebrating the Atlanta Jazz Festival

Central City Park: distaff

. . . and male preaching

Uniformed for the Hunter-Jumper Classic

Young woman and horse in casual Summer scene

Children with faces painted at Piedmont Arts Festival

Freshman indoctrination period at Emory

123

At the Kennesaw battlefield, the War is out of mind.

On the Chattahoochee, prepared for anything

124

Couple in Midtown at dogwood time

PHOTOGRAPHIC FOOTNOTES

p. 4: Georgia Plaza Park, State-financed, is a handsomely landscaped park with dining tables and underground parking. It is bordered by the Capitol, Atlanta City Hall and the Fulton County Courthouse complex. The original Immaculate Conception Church (not the building pictured) was one of the few structures spared by Gen. Sherman's troops during the burning of Atlanta.

p. 10: The spire is that of Second Ponce de Leon Baptist on Peachtree Road.

p. 11: The home, at 541 West Paces Ferry Rd., was built in 1926. It is one of several buildings in this volume designed by the distinguished Atlanta classical architect, Philip Shutze.

p. 14: The upper scene was shot at Oglethorpe University, the girl and marigolds at Lake Lanier Islands.

p. 16: The building seemingly in the clouds is Tower Place. For more detail, see note for p. 36.

p. 18: Above, Tullie Smith House, "plantation plain" in style, is more typical of an 1840 Georgia farmhouse than movies' columned mansions. It was moved from the present site of Executive Park at I-85 and North Druid Hills Rd. and restored on the grounds of the Atlanta Historical Society. Below, a restoration area in West End, a fashionable residential area launched in the 1870s; it subsequently fell on hard times.

p. 19: Scenes in Oakland Cemetery, which dates from 1850. Sculpture of children with umbrella was executed in the late 19th Century by J. L. Mott Ironworks. Lion of the fallen Confederacy is a copy of the famous Lion of Lucerne (Switzerland).

p. 20: Residence, Druid Circle, NE, Inman Park. In 1889 Atlantan Joel Hurt launched not only the Inman Park suburb but Atlanta's first electric streetcar linking it to downtown. In its heyday, the section was home of some of Atlanta's richest citizens. Over the years it became a slum, its once proud homes subdivided and neglected. But led by designer Robert Griggs in the late 1960s, Inman Park has been largely restored to its Victorian elegance.

p. 21: Atlanta became capital of Georgia in 1868. Its present Capitol was completed in 1889. The dome was gilded with Dahlonega, Ga., gold in the 1950s.

p. 22: Asa Candler, who turned an obscure local headache remedy called Coca-Cola into a nationally popular beverage, erected an office building for his various enterprises in 1906. Its lobby and exterior are handsomely ornamented with marble sculpture by F. B. Miles. The building was lovingly restored in the early 1970s.

p. 23: Philip Shutze designed Swan House in a blend of Baroque and Anglo-Palladian styles for the Edward Inman family. Completed in 1928, it is now part of the Atlanta Historical Society and its period-decorated rooms (see example, lower photo) are open to the public.

p. 24: The Georgia Governor's Mansion on West Paces Ferry Rd., NW, was completed in 1967. It is Greek Revival, a style popular with rich ante-bellum Southerners. Its public rooms are decorated with many fine pieces from the American Federal period (pre-1820).

p. 25: Philip Shutze introduced the Italian Baroque style to Atlanta in 1920 with The Villa Apartments on Montgomery Ferry Rd., NE (upper photo). His firm (Hentz, Adler and Shutze) also designed the luxurious Regency-style home (lower photo) at 320 West Paces Ferry Rd., NW.

p. 26: The fantasy world of the movies in their halcyon days inspired a fantasy Arabian Nights palace called the Fox Theatre. It opened in 1929 as a movie and stage house, and for many years was the setting of the annual Metropolitan Opera performances. It was destined for destruction but saved by an Atlanta Landmarks public campaign. It has proved a popular house for touring performers and is being restored.

p. 27: Two details from the short-lived Art Deco period: a bell-blazoned female figure on Southern Bell's Ivy Street building and elevator doors in the lobby of the William Orr Doctor's Building, 490 Peachtree St., NE.

p. 28: Architect John Portman revolutionized hotel design with the Hyatt Regency Atlanta, with its floor-to-roof atrium and space-capsule glass elevators.

p. 29: Art works and people-places are important elements in Portman's overall design for Peachtree Center. The upper photo is dominated by Charles Perry's fine stainless steel sculpture "Early Mace" Below, dining indoors in the Peachtree Center shopping mall and outdoors in front of the mall and South Building.

p. 30: The Atlanta Hilton, with the most rooms in the Southeast, offers outdoor glass elevator service (upper photo) to its rooftop lounge and fine Nikolai's Roof restaurant (architects: Wong & Tung, Mastin & Associates). Below, Portman's later hotel, the world's tallest, the 70-story Peachtree Plaza, has a "lake" in its complex lobby.

p. 31: Peachtree Summit has unique architectural answers to its unusual downtown site. It is directly tied to a MARTA subway station (architects: Toombs Amisano & Wells). This late afternoon scene was shot with a color filter.

p. 32: A gift from leading philanthropist Robert W. Woodruff made it possible to clear land for popular Central City Park, in the foreground. Tower in rear is striking Trust Company of Georgia headquarters, completed in 1968 (architects: Abreu & Robeson, with Carson Lundin & Shaw).

p. 33: The Georgia Power Building (architects: Finch Alexander Barnes Rothschild & Paschal), completed in 1961, helped set the tone for today's Peachtree Center area.

p. 34: Architects Thompson Ventulett Stainback & Associates designed all three of the Omni complex buildings, using weathering steel, glass and stone: the Coliseum, the Omni International megastructure and the Georgia World Congress Center. The first two are visible in the lower photo, with the Plaza Hotel in the distance and 101 Marietta Building at right. Above, interior of the megastructure with its two office wings, hotel, restaurants and retail shops.

p. 35: Several eras of architecture in late afternoon view of North Avenue. On skyline, l-r: Fox Theatre, Ponce de Leon Apartments, Peachtree North Apartments, "Tech Tower" at Georgia Tech, C&S North Avenue Tower (Aeck Associates, architects), Life of Georgia Tower (Lamberson Plunkett Shirley & Woodall, architects).

p. 36: Upper photo is Tower Place at sunset. The complex consists of a 29-story office tower (with 32 "corner" offices on the upper floors) and low-rise Tower Place Hotel, retail and recreational facilities (architects: Stevens & Wilkinson). Below, Colony Square (architects: Jova/Busby/Daniels)—exterior at left, enclosed connector and restaurant at right.

p. 38: Suburban office parks have been a significant trend in Metro Atlanta during the past decade-plus. Like this one (above), most are clustered along freeways. Atlanta home-buyers still are largely traditional in tastes. One of the few fine contemporary designs, pictured below, is the home of architect Joe Amisano.

p. 40: Hotels are keys to Atlanta's booming convention business, and competition is strong. This is view of pool and courtyard the downtown Marriott Motor Hotel recently enclosed. Roof is retractable.

pp. 44-45: Waiting line of jets ready for takeoff is familiar sight at busy Hartsfield (p. 44, above, all Eastern Airlines jets). The intricate movements are choreographed from the control tower shown by night on p. 45, above. Atlanta-based Delta Air Lines operates its jet fleet maintenance facility at Hartsfield (lower scenes, both pages).

p. 47: When C&S bought the old (1901) Empire Building in 1929, Philip Shutze redesigned the lower floors. The main banking room above was influenced by the Roman Pantheon. Below, models celebrate in Fox's Egyptian Ballroom after Yves St. Laurent showing. Atlanta's growing role in the fashion industry will be much enhanced by the new Apparel Mart in Peachtree Center.

p. 48: Atlanta is headquarters of the world-ranging Center for Disease Control.

p. 49: Atlanta Farmers Market (upper photo) is largest such facility in the world. Flea Market (lower) operates Fridays, Saturdays and Sundays at Piedmont Rd. and Lindbergh Dr., NE.

p. 50: Lockheed-Georgia in Marietta specializes in heavy-duty freight planes but also produces corporate jets. Western Electric, a major employer in the Metro area, produces cable at its Gwinnett County plant (below).

p. 51: Coca-Cola, born in Atlanta in 1886 as a fountain-dispensed headache remedy, has grown to an international, multi-product corporation based here. Bottling operations (lower photo) are independently operated franchises.

pp. 53-55: MARTA's rapid rail cars, manufactured in France by Franco-Belge, on rails at Avondale Yard (p. 53). Downtown's Five Points Station (pp. 54-55) is crossing point of East-West and North-South lines.

p. 57: Georgia World Congress Center (lower photos) has given enormous thrust to Atlanta's convention business. Its three-block-long exhibition hall is nation's largest on single level. It has auditorium and simultaneous translation facilities.

p. 63: Pictured is "Hoe-Downtown," part of Downtown Atlanta Days, a merchant-sponsored celebration.

p. 64: Pictured is a C&S employee picnic, a mere shadow of the madcap annual "Ramblin' Raft Race," sponsored by the American Rafting Association, Radio Station WQXI and others. It is Guinness-certified as the world's biggest participation sport.

p. 65: Pictured is one of several regattas on highly popular Lake Lanier. The golfing below is among many recreation activities available at the State-developed Lake Lanier Islands.

p. 66: Pictured is a scene from the Atlanta Track Club's annual Stone Mountain 1-, 5- and 10-mile races. The annual Fourth of July 6-mile Peachtree Road Race has grown to thousands of participants from all over the world.

p. 68: The scene is from "Play It Again, Sam."

p. 69: Burt's is one of several popular night spots in Omni International. It features "sets" from various movie hits. It's named for Burt Reynolds, who has made several movies in Georgia.

p. 70: The rhinos are in the "Lion Country Safari" part of Kingdoms 3, which also offers rides, live performances, picnic areas and nature trails (Stockbridge exit near Atlanta, I-75 South).

p. 71: Stone Mountain Park also has a skylift, train ride, water slides, a plantation complex, motel, restaurant and other diversions.

pp. 72-73: Besides the "Great Scream Machine" pictured, 276-acre Six Flags Over Georgia includes numerous other breathtaking rides, live entertainment, dining, etc.

pp. 74-76: This book was photographed during the months before the regular seasons of the Atlanta Flames (hockey) and Atlanta Hawks (basketball). Their limited appearance or nonappearance was unavoidable.

p. 80: Buckhead's St. Philip, Cathedral of the Episcopal Diocese of Atlanta, was born downtown in 1848; it's one of Atlanta's three oldest churches.

p. 82: In the Greek Orthodox Cathedral of the Annunciation, the striking panels by Sirio Tonelli represent (l-r): the Archangel Gabriel, the Annunciation, the Mother of God and the Divine Child, the Holy Gate, Christ, St. John the Baptist and the Archangel Michael.

p. 83: Second Ponce de Leon Baptist Church, now in Buckhead, is another of several churches which have moved with shifting residential patterns.

p. 84: The Temple is yet another example of Philip Shutze's classical style.

p. 85: The Monastery is operated by Trappist brothers.

pp. 86-87: Dr. King and his father, the Rev. M. L. King Sr., were co-pastors at Ebenezer Baptist Church. The tomb, p. 87, is part of Center which includes Dr. King's birthplace, Documentation Center, Community Center, Interfaith Chapel and walkway with historic scenes.

p. 90: Atlanta University is a graduate degree institution. Other components of the Atlanta University Center are Morehouse, Spelman, Morris Brown and Clark Colleges, and the Interdenominational Theological Seminary.

p. 94: The building at left houses administrative offices of Emory University's Woodruff Medical Center, one of the nation's outstanding medical facilities. It is named for Coca-Cola executive Robert W. Woodruff, whose contributions to Emory and the city have been extraordinary.

p. 95: Fernbank Science Center, operated by the DeKalb County Board of Education, has the nation's largest school-related planetarium, a major urban telescope, botanical gardens, a nature preserve, science museum, library and laboratories.

p. 96: Atlanta Memorial Arts Center houses the High Museum, Atlanta Symphony Orchestra, Alliance Theatre, Alliance Children's Theatre and Atlanta College of Art (architects: Toombs Amisano & Wells).

p. 98: The dancer here understandably is one of the photographer's favorite subjects: his partner, Judy Aycock.

p. 99: Glass sculptor Fräbel's works have been exhibited internationally. They frequently have been chosen as official gifts for visiting dignitaries.

pp. 100-102: Atlanta's Urban Wall murals are sponsored by the Arts Festival of Atlanta and Central Atlanta Progress, with funds from the National Endowment for the Arts. These examples are by Dale Pierson Hill (p. 100), Vee Brown (p. 101) and Larry Connatser (p. 102).

p. 103: Aeck Associates personnel created their own urban wall, balloons in relief, on one side of the architectural firm's building.

p. 108: The light sculpture, of aluminum and randomly flashing bands of colored neon, is by Boyd Mefferd.

p. 109: The aluminum sculpture (above) at the Midnight Sun is by Willi Gutmann. Below, Alexander Doyle's Henry W. Grady, honoring the great 1880s Atlanta Constitution Editor and apostle of an industrialized "New South."

p. 110: The eagle, above, is a bronze by Elbert Weinberg. Photographer used indoor film outdoors to achieve this color. The phoenix below, also a bronze, was executed by Gamba Quirino and was donated to the city by The Rich Foundation.

p. 122: The young woman is Rose Connell.

p. 123: The children with faces painted at the Piedmont Arts Festival are the photographer's godchildren, Kyle and Eric Frisch. The building shown below is typical of the "old" Emory campus.

p. 124: Running among the cannons is Judy Aycock. Below, inventor-engineer-manufacturer Larry Pierce of Douglasville is more serious than the pose suggests. He promotes tubing as cheaper, lighter and simpler than rafting, and has invented a bottom for comfort and safety. He holds the world's record for revolving in the tube: 1,050 turns in 21 minutes, eight seconds.

Notes of Thanks

The photographer thanks his gifted partner Judy Aycock for unending inspiration and her herculean effort in editing and organizing the massive number of color slides considered for this book; and his assistant Chuck Young, who handled the black-and-white printing.

The photographer and publishers are grateful to the scores of Atlantans without whose cooperation this project would not have been possible.

128